A Casino Bestiary

Poems by Denise Low

Kansas City Spartan Press Missouri

Spartan Press
Kansas City, Missouri
spartanpresskc.com

Copyright (c) Denise Low 2017
First Edition 1 3 5 7 9 10 8 6 4 2
ISBN: 978-1-946642-13-4
LCCN: 2017933599

Design, edits and layout: Jason Ryberg
Author photo: Stephan Anderson-Story
Cover image: Jaune Quick-To-See Smith
All rights reserved. No part of this publication may be reproduced or transmitted in any form or by any means, electronic or mechanical, including photocopying, recording or by info retrieval system, without prior written permission from the author.

ACKNOWLEDGMENTS

Prospero's Books and Spartan Press would like to thank Jeanette Powers, j.d.tulloch, Jason Preu, M. Scott Douglass, Shawn Pavey, Shawn Saving, Jesse Kates, Jim Holroyd, Steven H.Bridgens, Thomas Mason, Beth Dille, Mason Wolf, The West Plaza Tomato Co. and The Robert J. Deuser Foundation For Libertarian Studies.

Poems, sometimes in different forms, appeared in: *Blue Lyra Review:* "Garden of William Burroughs"; *Caprice:* "American Kama Sutra"; *Crafty Poet II* (Terrapin, 2016): "Casino Bestiary"; *Cream City Review:* "Jane's Maze"; *Fungi:* "Mythology"; *Gimme You Lunch Money: Heartland Poets Speak out against Bullies* (Palladin, 2016): "Music Lessons"; *I-70 Review:* "Commune Journal," "Buzzards at the Fairlawn Exit," "Muehlebach Hotel, Kansas City"; *Jackalope* (Red Mountain, 2016): "Chance: A Coyote Story," "Subliminal Tsi-s'du /Rabbit"; *Midwest Quarterly:* "Blue Jay," "Persimmons," "Woody Woodpecker"; *Thirty-Three* (Negative Capability, 2014), "Amaranth"; *New Letters:* "Bourne Conundrum," "Casino Bestiary"; *Numéro Cinq:* "Watermarks," "Imperfect Refraction"; *150 Kansas Poems:* "Forbidden"; *South 45 Blog:* "Dunce of Listicles"; *Summerset Review:* "Flight"; *Thorny Locust:* "Great Plains Riddles," "William Burroughs: His Alligator Snapper," "Sunflower Highway Postcards"; *Yellow Medicine Review:* "Andrew Jackson, I See You," "Questions for the Indian Casino Psychic"; *Zingara Blog:* "Remembering Monk."

CONTENTS

A Casino Bestiary / 1

Subliminal Tsi-s'du/Rabbit / 2

Imperfect Refraction / 3

Great Plains Riddles / 4

Amaranth / 6

Chance: A Coyote Story / 7

Bureau of Indian Affairs Meeting / 8

Bureau of Indian Affairs School, 1985 / 10

William S. Burroughs: His Alligator Snapper / 11

The Garden of William S. Burroughs / 12

Eye Riddles / 13

Persimmon Season / 16

Sunflower Highway Postcards / 17

Buffalo Country / 19

Woody Woodpecker, a.k.a. Pileated / 20

Buzzards at the Fairlawn Exit / 21

Mythology / 22

Grass Fire / 23

Black Scoters, Atlantic / 24

Santa Fe Novena / 25

Questions for the Casino Psychic / 26

Andrew Jackson, I See You / 27

Flight / 28

Meth: A Family Story / 29

Open Heart / 30

Watermarks / 31

4th Grade Class Photograph / 33

Music Lessons / 34

Remembering Monk, 1966 KC Jazz Festival / 35

Commune Journal / 37

Muehlebach Hotel, Kansas City / 39

Blue Jay / 40

Outline for an Abandoned Memoir / 41

American Kama Sutra / 43

Charlie Musselwhite Plays a Solo / 44

The Dunce of Listicles / 45

The Bourne Conundrum / 48

Forbidden / 49

The Heart Also Is a Sun / 50

Jane's Maze / 51

For my relatives, mentors, friends, enemies, neighbors, colleagues, editors, students:

I learn from all of you.

A Casino Bestiary

Wolverine triplets zing a match but one zags away.
Add dollars and shake hands with chrome handles.
Two yellow coyotes snarl and curl tails. Spin again.

A shaggy elk bull rises but stumbles downstream.
Add quarters and hear silver waterfalls tinkle.
Three rabbits disappear and appear and disappear.

Jaguar has a cameo role and departs grinning.
Add dimes and hear Wheel of Fortune ding-dong-ding.
Three honking geese fly in a line then falter.

White-tailed deer leap one after another after another.
Add buffalo nickels, buffalo nickels, buffalo nickels,
      buffalo nickels.
Prairie dogs on the screen swivel. Watch them vanish.

Subliminal Tsi-S'du/Rabbit

Just when your pants come off
Cottontail hops through the door.

Past tangled skirt and socks,
the rascal darts under the bed.

Voyeur in the dark, his ears
squirm. Claws retract.

He is snared in crisscross stories—
Su-li/Buzzard, Mister McGregor,

Easter eggs lost in churchyards.
How Grandmother taught him, *Stop!*

He freezes as moonlight unmasks you,
my own handsome man undressed.

Imperfect Refraction

This is your aging brain:
holograms flicker slivers,
images shimmy and fall
reconstituted as flash-dried

memories. This is what
it's like getting on in years.
Convex images pop alive.
Inner quick-pulsed screens

rerun Bre'r Rabbit, Tsi-s'tu,
Road Runner, high resolution
off-tilt, skewed-in-water eyes.
Peter Rabbit hops the fence.

Skype particles reassemble,
beam you back to a star-date
Osiris cruise on the Kaw,
that mud-bottom river of no return.

Great Plains Riddles

Junk cars
stagger down
Sand Creek Road.

Lightning flickers
rattler tongues
on windshields.

Gusts twang rusty
Aeolian harp
car springs.

Snake handlers
lie in graves
beyond the creek.

Nothing changes but
fire-opal suns by day
moonstones by night.

+
Whirlwind warrior Medicine Water
    and his woman Moki
ride fast horses, raise
    dustdevils in wheat fields.

Ghosts of the German family
spin the same trail
   black spirals backwards
running to a blood-stained sun.

+

Maybe a woman loved a Cheyenne man
   says the local legend.
Maybe a captive hanged herself on a willow.
Maybe her pale ghost walks at night.
Maybe moonlight's salt sprinkled on sand
   disappears into White Woman Basin.

Amaranth

Emerald fields spread
so vast they frighten Cortez.

Aztecs harvest seeds,
add honey, shape small gods.

Priests order the plants killed
yet sword fronds revive—

armed sentries around berries
crimson in noon sun.

After drought, leaves shrivel.
Stems palisade the creeks.

Their seeds ripen into hard
drops of Spanish blood.

Chance: A Coyote Story

I meet a tribal witch walking to class
at a school known for bad medicine.
I'm trying to reform, he says.
Think good thoughts. Get an education.
He studies ethnobotany. Flute classes.
He glances at me sideways.

Teachers are young grad students.
He pauses a heartbeat. Smiles.
His snout lengthens. His teeth flash.
Gaaaw, I say. *Take it easy on them.*
A bus whooshes past. His laughter
echoes from faraway canyons.

Bureau of Indian Affairs Meeting

Yellow-streaked coyotes sit together,
a few Albinos at the circle's edge,
and lean Grays loll around the north.

Alpha tells laughing hyena jokes.
All bare teeth in exaggerated grins.
Then real work begins —

budget appropriations
prey allocations and next
who gets fucked when and by whom

which forms to fill out for prey
which forms for fucking or being fucked
which for the golf trip to Albuquerque.

+
When the fight breaks out Grays
have the advantage eight to four.
Albinos huddle in the corner.
Yellows pile on the Gray Alpha

and tear at her throat. A Gray
breaks away and texts her tribal witch.
Soon lightning strikes the window.
In the eerie glow of the next bolt

Alpha howls as a blue snake
zigzags across the floor.
Everyone hops onto chairs until
the lights come back on.

+

The bell rings. Five o'clock.
Adjournment follows
Roberts Rules of Order—

ass-sniffing in the usual sequence,
GS-11s first round, GS-12s
and so forth to the Alpha

howling from the highest spot
of the largest pile of shit.

Bureau of Indian Affairs School, 1985

After class the library director assigns girls to help with textbooks. They must wear skirts.

The Native powwow sponsor takes his pick. By Thanksgiving, three girls go home pregnant. At the spring powwow relatives of the girls give the sponsor black eyes for regalia.

One teacher fails thousands—no one good enough.

Another tells students how dumb they are.

Another gives everyone A's and leaves campus each morning by ten.

Another leaves after lunch to teach at another college.

Ceiling tiles are made of asbestos. Water fountains carry lead-laced water. Walls hide black mold. Radon glows in building foundations.

William S. Burroughs: His Alligator Snapper

An alligator snapping turtle raises
her bald hood through pond water.
She untangles her neck, reconnoiters,
heaves ashore like a jon boat.
She carries weapons—sabered beak,
back-ridges, taloned feet—
affixed to her body like Burroughs,
who carried a knife or derringer
or a solidified whale's penis
as a walking stick.

The turtle makes for the creek,
claws scoring slashes in the grass.
She slides gently down the bank,
tilts, returns to primal mud.
The spell vanishes like an avatar's
incarnation or last night's squall.
The place falls silent again
but everything feels different as though
a tornado lifted away but next time
will remember the address.

The Garden of William S. Burroughs

Poison ivy pokes mitts
through orgone-box slats.
Elderberry hedges stand guard.

A back yard pond frames
scrim of algae scum. Koi lurk.
Arrowroot leaves are hatchets.

*In the afternoons he might
walk in the garden and practice
his knife throwing.*

A smaller pool — moon-round,
cattail-circled bracken —
reflects outside his window.

At night dank water ripples
as fingers loosen grip
on his titanium Colt revolver.

Eye Riddles

Laser-dot red eyes among green
euonymus sheaves:
    A vireo darts herky jerky
    on spliced-video film.
    Looped once, looped twice:
    Tweet. Silence. Tweet. Silence.

+

Peony buds drip sap
    striped billiard balls
    red white green white
    eyes squeezed shut.

+

Lookout chipmunk:
    its kohl-lined eyes
    point the way
    past pine's
    bare slash.
    Tail taut
    black bead eyes
    look
    out.

\+

A cat's vertical eyes
>	are tandem gyroscopes
>	level just so.
>	Its body circles
>	unmoved elliptical
>	twin stars.

\+

Dog eyes are brown honey
>	traps.

\+

Snake eyes
>	slit yellow moonlight
>	make two wires
>	skewering
>	tossed ivory
>	cubes.

\+

Kelly green poison veins
>	feed on plump potato flesh.

>	Below nubby eye bumps
>	Cuzco-line alien lifeforms glow.

\+
What
> my father
> saw that night
> the door jamb
> painted
> Evil Eye
> in invisible ink.
> He tells me
> *The Devil is real.*

Persimmon Season

Pick tiny orange suns
before nightfall.

Their mummy-wrinkled heads
grin.

Clotted flesh is soft enough
to spoon.

Mix pulp into
sweet batter.

The oven stokes cinnamon
tumescence.

Butter and taste. Exchange
wet kisses.

Sunflower Highway Postcards

Two-Headed Cow
says the highway sign
                but look
a six-legged cow is the one
                alive.
Her extra hooved feet
                protrude
from her side awkward as her
                udder
eyes round and blank as
                creek stones.

+

Semis hurtle through wind tunnels
    teetering boxes lunging to Denver
    back to Chicago through Wichita
    laded stacked counted weighed.

Drivers in small cabs up high
    watch *Smokey and the Bandits*
    call code names on radios
    jostle in passing lanes

    hustle loads to everywhere
    getting nowhere but back where
    they started—small town sheds
    with giant trucks parked alongside.

\+
Tough stems
> claw hardpan dirt
> sing no tunes
> in ceaseless wind.

Yellow rosettes rise
> > roots clenching bedrock where
> > > bayonets rot orange
> > > flint knives splinter.

Buffalo Country

I ask the rancher *What's her name?*
He says, *Number Thirty-four.*

No joking. *She's a good grazer.*
Jumped the fence a coupla times.

He spits tobacco juice, adds,
Her calves always have good weight.

The shaggy female's black eyes gleam.
Her tail switches like a snake about to strike.

Beyond electric wire, the bull glowers.
Auburn yearlings clump in bluestem.

The mother lowers her horns, grazes.
Talk turns to the price of winter wheat.

Woody Woodpecker, A.K.A. Pileated

Hardly gone, he barely returns.
Evasive, yes, but red crest,
hammer beak, and whoops are distinct.
All know such a character—
the quiet one flamboyantly dressed.

Resurgence continues, migration
across the Missouri, a quiet shift.
Like cougars and armadillos,
the pileateds reappear stealthily.
They hollow out hidden nests.

Against canopy gloom
coxcomb plumage flickers
into focus and just as quickly
blurs. The bird is a half-myth,
a has-been actor in a lost cartoon.

Buzzards at the Fairlawn Exit

Black-plumed lords glide
Xibalba's realm of Mayan hell—
exhaust fumes of Topeka.

Kettling shadows lap asphalt.
Squirrels trip under tires.
Possums are squashed flat.

Buzzard wings laze figure 8s.
Their dot-eyes spot morsels.
They gather, crouch, and gorge.

Rot simmers in their guts.
Daily the dark flock performs
these Buddhist sky burials.

Elsewhere they bury their own dead
in private rituals. Each year
their generations repeat.

Mythology

The giant dozes under a hickory tree.
Above, leaves turn ripe yellow,
ginger, dismal brown. They fall.

Snow drifts over, wind blows.
May's morels finally poke through,
wrinkled toes of a forgotten ogre.

Grass Fire

A rattler races
        smoke's frenzy.

Red-tailed hawks
tastes blood's
sour tang.

Twilight chars
        stubble.

Cinder stars
        dot an exploding sky.

Black Scoters, Atlantic

India ink black
Hebrew letters
overlay mists.

Aleph downstrokes
mark fast script—
black scoters

skimming rip-tide
choppy wavelets
dodging dawn wind

scrawling one flock-
length Sabbath.
Then confusion.

Santa Fe Novena

Saltillo tiles skein quick
       shivering filaments of rain.

Thin lizard bones and cholla needles—
rosaries of August—spiral gullies.

Cloud banks unstack themselves behind
       the low-set moon.

Earth's many gods stand above:
       Lupus, Taurus, Ursus, Serpens.

Questions for the Casino Psychic

I've had eight back surgeries.
At night I dream I'm flying with blood-
soaked wings. When will this end?

I have pain from fibromyalgia.
At night I hear my voice call to angels.
Who answers me?

We hear loud steps on the stairs
and find clothes thrown to the floor.
Can you make the ghosts leave our house?

My three daughters are gone.
Why do their pictures on the mantle
change places each time I look away?

My son and his friend died hunting.
They froze in a blizzard. This winter,
is it their dogs I hear howling from the river?

My husband and children burned to death
in our house. Only the baby survived.
She is nineteen. Will she be all right?

Tomorrow at Mill Pond
a teenager will beat her sister to death.
Do you know about this? Can you stop it?

Andrew Jackson, I See You

I spindle, wad, and trade you for tens
but banks dispense more of your face—
flaring hair, horsey face, sharp cheeks,
arrogant look of moral rightness.

I see an outlaw who betrayed Creeks,
double-crossed the Supreme Court,
seized Cherokee farms and gold mines,
and ordered many Trails of Tears.

Today your bills are common trash.
Americans everywhere squash you,
squat walleted butt-cheeks over you,
cram you into purses with tissue.

Cell phones clang in your big ears,
bartenders spill whiskey up your nose,
sloppy eaters smear you with fries,
kids deface you with ink disguises.

New Orleans nuns saved you for this
afterlife of paper zombie confetti.
Users roll you and snort dope. Still,
Andy, this hell is far too good.

Flight

Fast
this crawling
water serpent
doubling the Missouri
state line
called
the Big Muddy.

I remember
the Kickapoo man
named for a death
march crossing.
Soldiers watched
children drown.
His grandfather
lived.

I remember
Mississippi
/*Jessepe*
his life
his great river
still rising
so powerful
no army can
halt it.

Meth: A Family Story

After bullets leave dead my niece
        and the drug dealer boyfriend

crows scream at her only brother.
Hidden in palm trees, birds repeat alarms.

He reads the papers, "Unidentified bodies
        found shot at Lake Elsinore."

Across the Ortegas their mother waits.
She knows this day is coming—

        back page news, boldface headlines,
        trickster voices loud in the trees.

That night dogs bark at sudden wind.
Fog persists. Brother turns the ignition,

        reverses out the driveway. By noon
        he will tell their mother.

Another death begins the moment
        she tips a fourth jigger of scotch.

She lasts a year and some months.
The killer gets a hard twenty.

Few remember her name. Lisa Frances.
These black letters outline her corpse.

Open Heart

The surgeon scores the breastbone with a flat-edge blade and cuts. The heart, a wild animal, accelerates until set free.

Obsidian-sharp steel slices bloody arteries, precise slits by a man who, another time, might be an Aztec cutting out a heart or a Viking turning a foe into a blood eagle.

The un-hearted body lies in a cold room for six hours. The gore is spot-lit. Downward swipes of the knife do not reverse.

In the next room a woman knits a herringbone fate, stitch and purl, as the surgeon pierces tiny sutures through a muscle knot. He loops wire thread, cobbling human skin and bone. Delicate coils secure tunnels before they course with blood and jitters of electricity.

The surgeon packs his tools. Orderlies wheel a sedated corpse down a long hall and set the brake.

He lies unmoving for a day.

When he finally speaks, he will tell nobody what he has seen.

Watermarks
(Kenneth Lee Irby, 1936-2015)

You no longer "care" for anything to eat
except sweet brandy

>   A last bottle
>   yes, I bought it
>   and I'm not sorry

You sip
slumped sideways on the sofa
>   bracket of spine tilting

fever-red cheeks
>   the marionette lines barely
>   holding you up

long-sleeved denim shirt
>   over skin so thin

blue veins shine
>   bones jut the collar

+

Like a fool I bring
Japanese fairy tales—
>   my father's book
>   rich slick mildewy paper

Your overgrown thumbnail slits open pages
Through your hands tumble

        persimmons
        red foxes
        yellow-lantern moons
+
A blood moon rises overhead
full in Leo, not Scorpio

The mud knot of your heart
        loosens its jagged dithyrambs

For good-bye I lay hands
on your blanket-swaddled chest
feel it   that swell
unspindling

4Th Grade Class Photograph

Not a bouquet of gray roses
but whorl faces in tiered rows
evenly spaced on folding chairs:
Anita next to Linda Sue, alive here
before leukemia, and Alan before
Vietnam. Cynthia's calm eyes
in eternal madonna repose.

We are clocks with years coiled
to this set point. All of us stare,
timekeepers of small dramas
for an audience of doting parents
lost in the expanse of decades.
Our myriad grandchildren breathe
outside this frame of shadows.

Beside the risers looms Killer
Keller, meanest teacher of all.
No one knows her Christian name.
Tight curls line a domed head.
Her face clenches, no smile.
She looks past the photographer
to the place where I now stand.

Music Lessons

Fourteen and developed,
I am a morsel trapped
in the music studio.
He never lays a hand on me
but after my wheezy scales
he smirks about blow jobs.

In the Army he liked
whores. *Sex,* he says,
is rubbing sticks together.
I play "Take Five"
as his fingers drum
the rhythm by my face.

His girlfriend is country,
raw-boned, soft-spoken.
When I'm sixteen
we all drive to Kansas City
in his big gray Chrysler.
This is how I get to see Thelonious.

Remembering Monk, 1966 Kc Jazz Festival

Thelonious two-steps
stage edges

the drummer
thumps a solo

the bass player
hums.

Monk jigs back backwards
to the bench

spreads fingers
stares at them

riffles an arpeggio
deck of cards

clunks two
notes together

stops for cymbals
dances

prowls behind curtains
comes back. Sits.

Outlines a rattler spine
of notes

"Bemsha
Swing."

Walks offstage
maybe gone

gone maybe
or not.

Commune Journal

Fridays we watch Alan Watts Zen on TV while Craig polishes motorcycle chrome. Existentialism is tonight's word.

Bill dries ditch-weed in the oven. He sells bales of it to California dealers for filler.

Saturday nights we knot dry cleaner's plastic, dangle the mashed crinkles from the porch beam, and set fire—a fizzling green-flame zilch.

A disassembled harpsichord litters the parlor floor. We trip over brass strings.

On Halloween, the back-yard tire swing smells of asphalt. In the cupboard we find only pancake mix for supper.

One winter night I sit alone on the dusty oak floor. By candlelight, I read Pericles and weep.

Police bring a homeless teen for shelter. He tells astral projections stories. He tells about a fire that lasted all night after the wood burned to ash.

Spring comes. Bill assembles the harpsichord, sells it, and pays the rent before police arrest him in his loincloth.

Perry packs his occult library and bicycles to Utah, where he once turned Jack Kerouac onto mescaline.

I continue typing Professor Lind's German translations of the *Iliad*. I understand neither Greek nor German.

The downstairs boy never tells us his name. When violets bloom he enlists in the Navy. The morning he leaves for Vietnam he drops acid and blasts "Here Comes the Sun."

The rest of us change clothes, put on shoes, and walk out the front door. No one remembers to lock it.

Muehlebach Hotel, Kansas City

The red-faced clerk leans over the counter
leering at my breasts. My groom stutters.
I grab the single brass key.

Carved ivy vines trim the staircase.
Globe lighting sheds nightmare tints
muting sofas and walnut wainscoting.

The elevator man speaks minor-key tunes.
His flat eyes are quarter-notes of silence.
The door heaves shut and we ascend.

The final lurch turns my stomach.
We clamber out of the vertical tunnel
to our room of ginger jar lamps.

We sit speechless in gloom. Midnight,
I scrutinize gray windows. In the lobby
Hemingway types tomorrow's paper.

Blue Jay

I could be that pesky jay
scraping air with whiskey voice,
eavesdropping from a branch.
I could jeer at your half-kiss
broken off and the quick slam
gravelly cough and stutter
of starter, screaming tires spun
on asphalt and you're gone.

I could follow you on River Road
until dark and then exude
flute notes like blue jays gargle
hidden in our yews. I could
hover and comment, *sotto voce,*
praising failed love's release.

Outline For An Abandoned Memoir

First, 38 degrees north and 78 degrees west: Flint Hills of Kansas roll under videogame brick streets. Moths mob strobing streetlights. Slow analog clocks tick. First summer. Chapter 1.

Books at the center: Edgar Rice Burroughs and Tarzan, Robert E. Howard and Conan. Kipling, Twain. My grandmother's Rexroth and Li Po, Tu Fu.

Chapter 3 will be Herodotus, Thucydides, Sophocles, Aeschylus. Handwritten Greek verbs went places without me. I was the worst student in class.

Another axis: stories I hear from the Cherokee man Hal Gibson. He teaches Sunday school as community service but really tells stories about Chino prison guards, his jazz career in L.A., and how heroin kicked his ass.

Interiors, next chapter. The basement apartment of brown tile, pine-paneled walls, thin-legged recluse spiders. A tiny kitchen but clean. Periscope light from windows. My Pawnee landlady hosts '49 gatherings as I sleep to drumming and singing overhead.

Each house is an exoskeleton.

Chapter 9, the food: My mother's asparagus patch and the asparagus I planted in 1977. Open-air food markets in Thailand with buckets of braided eels alive. We eat on the *soi* at Uncle's stall, his drunken noodles. Tom's pork roast. His ceviche. My son makes wine in Sonoma County and hears all its colors. Dino in D.C., Little Serow, Pachamama's, Tellers, Scopa, and Bert's Drive-in with salty loose hamburger scooped into buns.

Chapter 10 I reveal most of these places are gone.

Music teachers: The kind piano teacher across the street but I cried anyway. The professor who asked each week if I were still a virgin. The other one who tried to change that.

What got me through: Stravinsky's *Rites of Spring*, an old '78 my father had, and its thick, shiny plastic revolving on a spindle straight as a bolt.

Xavier Cugat, Fats Waller, Duke Ellington, Charlie Christian. Thelonious. Trane. Cannonball. Paul Desmond and Dave Brubeck.

The Creek Stomp dance in Stidham Union with voices resounding all night calling ancestors into this time.

Last chapter: I could go on.

American Kama Sutra

Pose 1
On the floor
origami sheets fold
into a giant naked
Bear.

Pose 2
Tomorrow it's my turn
with the red cowboy boots.

Pose 3
I've learned a lot about your people
living with you,
my lover says,
his leg thrown over
my smooth ass.

Pose 4
Tell me again.
Today,
who's fucking whom?

Charlie Musselwhite Plays a Solo

Builds a house of twelve-bar blues
with broken steps, *The bell just toned,*
my baby done caught that train

and gone—a trapdoor where he tumbles
to hellfire. Flames lick his steel harp.
He cries so hard his pain burns.

He yowls until all he has left is
starlight sugar sweetening night,
The bell just toned, my baby caught

that train. Sinning never sounded so good,
Everything happening, I am to blame—
pitiful angel, fallen so far down
he's all the way up.

The Dunce Of Listicles

1. In a 1970s poetry class I read "Thirteen Ways of Looking at a Blackbird" and begin writing numbered, sectioned poems.

2. In 2014 I discover *listicle,* the word for numbered, sectioned trivia like "Five Ways to Shampoo Your Poodle" and "Eight Origami Folds for Trash Sacks." A fellow writer tells me she makes a good income teaching "How to Write Listicles" workshops.

3. In 2008 I find one of my early books of numbered, sectioned poems in a used bookstore, inscribed to a fr/enemy. Every poet in town goes to this bookstore, so this private gesture is a public announcement. This is a brilliant passive-aggressive coup.

4. In 2009 at the same bookstore I discover one of my books of poems marked in red ink. In the front leaf I see this assignment was due March 8 for the Advanced Poetry Class. Only on the last page is there faint praise— *The image of wheeling Orion works okay.*

5. I do not have enough cash to buy this book and burn it. I decide to let it travel through the time listicle known as the calendar.

6. In 2010 my new book of numbered, sectioned poems arrives in the mail. On the first page I realize the printer cut off the last section.

7. The poem works better without it.

8. In 1984 I take my children to the special collections library to find a review of my numbered, sectioned poem sequence. The librarian gives the kids free pencils and brings the review. The unsectioned prose praises the typography, handmade paper, and abstract designs derived from quilt patterns—but finds my poems lackluster. The children use the stubby library pencils to draw sad faces on milk cartons.

9. The same day the mail carrier brings a rejection letter for a numbered, sectioned poem. Rejection always comes in listicles.

10. This one says, *The T'Ang poets already did what you are attempting badly. Give it up.* I burn the letter. Later, I regret its loss because when I tell the story, no one believes it is true.

11. It is true.

12. In 2015 I realize everything I write is a listicle, snaking through the bowel of Mother Wormhole, like Stephen Hawking's arrow of time only wriggling forward in eel-like motions. Sometimes pages are unnumbered. Sectioned episodes of my existence disappear into the white page beyond all listicles.

13. I wake up in pure air of 1970 and hear blackbirds call my name thirteen times.

The Bourne Conundrum

A rusted escape ladder gives way. I fall behind.
Paris police reach the brownstone corner
but the CIA chases me past headquarters. I jack

a cruiser with sirens, 360 it in the parking lot.
Cops get closer. I turn fifty years old, still steering
as enemy agents gain ground. Snow drifts turn icy.

She drove off the roof, a fat man says into a phone
but no mention of cancer. I awaken at night. Reset
the game. I wheel a green Mustang, slapping hills,

squealing rubber. Skewer an airborne turn,
slide to the ditch and teeter. The Dodge explodes.
I'll keep her in play one trenchcoat says to another.

No one tells me about the assassination program
until I see my *Wanted* profile on the news, crash
a window, pivot, and toss down a bag of passports.

It lands by a video-game gangster. He grabs it
for points. At the East River I dive through blue air—
a final maneuver while the Coast Guard closes in.

I stare into the surveillance camera: *Why me?*
but no answer. Screens flicker back into play.

Forbidden

He pulls fear from a wooden drawer—
        an Aboriginal witching stone
        given to his uncle years ago.

As he unwraps flannel swaddling he says,
        unflinchingly unsexing me,
Women should not see this taboo.

He holds the pecked lodestone to light,
        a Gondwanaland lava remnant
        at first unremarkable but magnetic,

the white-on-black pattern:
spiral galaxy
        foaming river eddy
        my own rosette labia exposed.

The Heart Also Is A Sun

A bonfire where grief burns
        Rage bellows scarlet

Where Sirens spin searing whorls
        flesh rises from magma

Lightning strikes flint sparks
        Breath cools the embers

Caged by bone and damped by blood
        its perpetual combustion

        launches solar flares within, below:
        U-ne-la-nv-hi

Jane's Maze

Go North on River Road past
shallows lined with eagles.

Turn East on Wellman where creeks
trip step-stone hills.

Pink granite erratics dot
sloping pastures. Keep going

past Dabinawa to the road's T.
Turn South into the dead end.

Saplings circle the shrine,
stone in center, fire to the West,

terra cotta basin of water,
Celtic cross of bronze—

Irish medicine wheel.
Enter from the East.

NOTES

"Subliminal Rabbit/Tsi-s'du" includes Cherokee words for Rabbit and Buzzard.
"Imperfect Refraction" is for Roger Holden, a Lawrence, Kansas, genius who works with hologram communications. *Kaw* is a local term for the Kansas River. Thanks to Otto Preminger et alia for the *River of No Return* line (1954).
"Great Plains Riddles" refers to conflict between Cheyenne and settler families, 1874.
William S. Burroughs poems are informed by stories of Thomas King and Wayne Propst, generously shared, as well as my own 1990s visits. Wilhelm Reich developed the idea of an orgone box.
The quotation is from Barry Miles, *Call Me Burroughs*.
"Buzzards at the Fairlawn Exit" refers to Xibalba, Mayan hell. Dennis Etzel asked me for a Topeka poem.
"Questions for the Casino Psychic" has origins in Sylvia Browne's appearance at the Menominee Casino.
"Open Heart Surgery" is for Linda Rodriguez, who knits and sits with friends.
"Commune Journal" is for Bill Butler with gratitude for funding a year of my (misspent) youth.
"Forbidden" is for Barnaby Ruhe, on the death of Ed Ruhe, collector of Australian Aboriginal art (Kluge-Ruhe Aboriginal Art Collection, University of Virginia).

Denise Low, second Kansas Poet Laureate, is award-winning author of 25 books of prose and poetry, including *The Turtle's Beating Heart: One Family's Story of Lenape Survival* (University of Nebraska); *Jackalope* (short fiction, Red Mountain); *Mélange Block* (poetry, Red Mountain); *Ghost Stories* (Woodley, a Kansas Notable Book; The Circle-Best Native American Books); and *Natural Theologies: Essays* (Backwaters Press). She edited a selection of poems by William Stafford in an edition with essays by other poets and scholars, *Kansas Poems of William Stafford* (Woodley). Low is past board president of the Associated Writers and Writing Programs. She blogs, reviews, and co-publishes Mammoth Publications. She teaches professional workshops nationally as well as classes for Baker University's School of Professional and Graduate Studies.

www.ingramcontent.com/pod-product-compliance
Lightning Source LLC
Chambersburg PA
CBHW021452080526
44588CB00009B/811